WATERMELON KINDNESS

WATERMELON KINDNESS

DAVID DONNELL

MISFIT

ECW Press

Published by ECW Press
2120 Queen Street East, Suite 200, Toronto, Ontario, Canada M4E 1E2
416.694.3348 / info@ecwpress.com

LIBRARY AND ARCHIVES CANADA CATALOGUING IN PUBLICATION

Donnell, David, 1939-
Watermelon kindness / David Donnell.

Poems.
ISBN 978-1-55022-914-1

I. TITLE.

PS8557.O54W38 2010   C811'.54   C2009-905967-3

Editor for the press: Michael Holmes / a misFit book
Cover and text design: Tania Craan
Author photo: John Frederick Eddington
Cover images: Water Melon Slice With Bites © Carole Gomez / iStockphoto
Wood planks on black © Maria Toutoudaki / iStockphoto
Typesetting: Mary Bowness
Printing: Coach House   1   2   3   4   5

This book is set in Centaur MT

The publication of *Watermelon Kindness* has been generously supported
by the Canada Council for the Arts, which last year invested $20.1 million in writing and publishing
throughout Canada, by the Ontario Arts Council, by the Government of Ontario through the
Ontario Book Publishing Tax Credit, by the OMDC Book Fund, an initiative of the Ontario
Media Development Corporation, and by the Government of Canada through the
Book Publishing Industry Development Program (BPIDP).

Canada Council   Conseil des Arts   Canadä   ONTARIO ARTS COUNCIL
for the Arts   du Canada   CONSEIL DES ARTS DE L'ONTAR

PRINTED AND BOUND IN CANADA

ECW PRESS
ecwpress.com

This book is for Sidney Crosby, who played so well during the 2010 Vancouver Olympics. We were finalizing the very last pages of *Watermelon Kindness* during the last weekend of the games. Crosby was all over the place helping other people against Slovakia, without scoring the big stat himself. Then, tied up 2–2 in overtime against the Americans, he scored. A huge, deliberate goal. A role model. For sure. Hey, guy, you did it.

I'm standing by the window where the light is strong
— Leonard Cohen, *Tower of Song*

CONTENTS

LIFE STYLES

Mariner 3

At the Café de Kahlua on West St. Clair 4

Iraq 5

Obama's iPod 6

A Poet in the Kitchen 7

Watermelon Kindness 8

It Was Before Your Time 9

The Truth 10

Life Enthusiasts 11

Breaking Up with Miriam Mulstein 12

Platforms 13

Poems I've Thought of Writing 15

Your Effulgence Disorients Me 16

Facing the Streetcars 17

Drunken Horses 19

Scarlett Johansson 20

Watermelon Summer 21

Poetry Reading, Oak Park, Ill. 22

Behold the Lillies of the Field 23

Remember Sean? 25

In/Out 26

Titles 27

It's Lonely at the Top 28

A Comic Moment Toward the End of a Serious Relationship 29

A Slightly Stoned Descartes 30

Bright Red Numbers on a Digital Morning Clock 31

Grants 32

Lateral Interference in Daily Life 33

I'm Not Walking in Circles 35

She Thinks Zen Is Too Intellectual 37

Ibid. 38

Wills 39

On Getting Over a Depression 40

Book City on a Saturday Morning 41

Neu Gedichte 42

People Who Make the Scene 44

How to Become a Better Person 45

Dismissiveness 47

Are Most of Us a Little Crazy? 48

10 Reasons Not to Buy a Smart Car 49

How to Save Your Life 50

Dizzy 52

TAKE ME TO THE RIVER

To Die For 55

Djuna Barnes 56

Accounting 58

I Guess Baseball Players Wear Baseball Caps 60

ABC 61

Marco Polo in China 62

Fuses 63

Kansas 64

Did Blavatsky Ever Meet Edward VII? 65

Legzzz 67

Fluid Motion 68

Spreading the Word 69

The Nature of Language 70

Kiev Is Dark at Night and Very Historic. They Have Warm Lakes to
    the South. 71

Unforgettable Men 73

Some Shocks Are Delicious 74

Well-educated Well-read Young Writer Who Can't Finish His First
    Novel Because He's Obviously Distracted 75

Jack 76

Cool 77

Traffic 78

The 2 Giovannis 80

Free Fall 81

October 82

Men 83

OBAMA POEMS

George the 3rd Plus His Madness 87

The Differences Between Us 88

Obama Campaigning 90

Pre-emptive Strike 91

The Significance of State 93

Midwestern, Leaning East to Seaboard 97

Little Moron 99

Bruce's Yams 100

An NFB Full of Luminous Still Photographs 102

Blue Skies & Opera 106

Jaffa Oranges Are Sweet 108

Amazing & Innocent 110

Caricature 111

Driving All the Way to Tibet 113

You 115

Trends That Didn't Start in America 116

Painters Who Were Not Exactly Put Out of Business by Jackson
        Pollock's Relative Success in 1942 118

The Great Philosophers Don't Listen to Enough Coltrane 119

Computer Files 120

Rust Never Sleeps 121

Afrika/Afrique 122

A Couple of Interesting Brothers 124

Geraldine 125

Gerald Murphy 126

North of 60 128

Einstein & Daily Life 130

LIFE STYLES

Mariner

Mariner is circling Hubble. And I am
down here
writing a poem about a pear. Thinking about my life,
naturally,
how specific incidents
like lost money, or a broken love affair, or political disappointment
have often led me to lose perspective.

A ripe yellow pear lying on a saucer over on the kitchen counter.
How simple a form & how its perfect ripeness is
a metaphor for any given moment of love in an open field.

The largeness of the world is
when you stop to think about it
unthinkable. It is large beyond large. Largeness beyond
largesse. There are galaxies beyond
the sun and each day the sun is a gift. Here over a million miles
away I am much larger than my furniture, this pear is a gift, I split it open
it is fresh & white & sweet its brown shiny seeds bright with pectin.

At the Café de Kahlua on West St. Clair

We didn't realize for a split second, did we,
Abner,
            sitting in that cute little Café de Kahlua late at night
with all the darkness of west St. Clair around us well outside,

that people's minds can change completely
like a Marilyn Monroe look-alike getting tired of sex poses,

or a guy who drinks too much & insults his friends
suddenly waking up on a sunny morning & saying, Mr. Dewar's,

I'm kissing you & your white label off like a bad first date.

Do you remember that wonderful large poster from the Spoleto
Jazz
            Festival on the wall just where you had to make a little
turn & then go downstairs to the john. Great poster. Made me

want to go to Italy, & now you've been 3 times & I haven't.

And the red-haired Italian guy — a real shock of real red —
who was usually reading
a book about something or other — behind the Gaggia espresso
machine.

4

Iraq

I can't imagine, get through to, batter my head against the
glass wall of the Baghdad Arrivals level — of course I'm not there,
don't be foolish, almost no one except authorized personnel & authorized
visitors are there — what the U.S. hopes to achieve
by staying in Iraq year after bloody year. Obviously they're not going
to convert the fairly large population to left-wing Catholicism. Obviously.
For sure they are not going to convert to Orthodox Buddhism. Sunnis remain
Sunni & Shiite remain Shiite or Shia. Does the State Department hope
To achieve total possession of all the oil tracts & contracts of the
'50s & '40s? Are these questions going to come up in international court —
I suppose that means in the Hague — but we're not being told about it
Until NBC or CBS or CNN need a whole series of features. Something like
"Slit skirt comes back in 2012" *or* "Pumps with a dot of colour are the new
thing." The war has cost America a fortune. Some people in specific industries
have made a fortune. Peaceniks have demonstrated outside of airports. Howard
Dean lost his candidacy because of the scream. He screamed at the end of his
Iowa speech. I don't know. Was it Iowa? Do I give a fuck? Do I give a
flying fuck in a tin can? I don't know. Why don't they just station some special
killer F-22s at a special airport around Kirkuk & ipso facto bring the troops home?

Obama's iPod

I don't think Obama   president elect
& of whom many & various great things are expected,
is really going to dig this Canadian iPod all that much.
— 49 pieces of music
— not 49 states before Hawaii
but 49 as in the 49th parallel.
I sort of dig it, but you know, not really, not *really*,
most of us live south of the 49th parallel,
however it's the *idea* that counts
& let's face it, Chuck, the *idea* is cute, it holds water,
it's doable. *So*, what have we got?
Glenn Gould playing the *Goldbergs*, nobody seems to care
if it's the '55 or the '81, k.d. lang singing Cohen's *Hallelujah*
O there are some unexpected treats,
Maureen Forrester singing *ombra mai fou* from Handel's *Xerxes*,
tasty stuff, is there any way we can get Owen Pallett
in there with all the Gould & Brueggergosman?

A Poet in the Kitchen

"B, i, n, d, a, e." He spells each letter of the Korean word,
then,
      t-shirt flapping around his elbows
& much to the discreet amusement of his pretty
girlfriend,
also Korean
naturally, it's a Korean auction sale for the Bloor United Church
then
as I've said before
he flaps both arms, "like a duck," he says, "like a duck."
O, I say,
I get it.
      "Bin dae duk, right," he says. It's a very wonderful
Korean pancake made with ground mung beans, onion strands, garlic,
& several other gorgeous items.

Watermelon Kindness

A pleasant summer, walk up through Hillsdale to St. Clair,
so many side streets you could use a city directory.

A boy about 10 or so & a girl maybe 2 years younger.
A plank & 2 industrial cartons. "FreSH WaterMelon, 25¢."

I stop for a moment & ask them how good it is. He pauses
& then says, "It's fresh." So I give him 50¢. It's a
nice big piece. A round really, but gorgeous.

The first bite full of juice. This is what kindness should be like.
My throat was dry, the watermelon concession was unexpected.

Kindness should stun us with the simplicity of a perfect moment.

O come on let me pick up the cheque is sometimes a little overdone.

Can you watch my bike just for a second I'll be right back.
Well, okay, at least that's sincere.

Surprise is a part of kindness. I'll take this one.

The Megalopolis is still a city with some amazing neighbourhoods.
I enjoyed the presentation as much as the cool sweet taste.

It Was Before Your Time

It was before your time. Surely you could look it up for me,
it's a 1976 book,
it may be in reprint. Beethoven's *Sonata No. 3*, a bit obscure,
no, all the top players love the final movement
of that early sonata. That was before your time.

Thomas Pynchon & the new American novel, before your time,

William Faulkner & the new American novel, before your time,
David Bowie's first LP, *Hunky Dory*, good title, before your time,
the invention of the dildo, that was definitely before *Giulio Cesare*,
the Wright brothers, doomed to be birds, born to fly, before, *plus ultra*,
the Toronto subway system, definitely before your time,
Neil Armstrong walks on the moon,
O, One great step for mankind — well, it was for Michael Jackson,
before your time,
Jaws, by the very talented Steven Spielberg, before, your time,
The Tin Drum, by Günther Grass, before, different country, a novel,
bah,
motherfucker,
the Ossington bus, you know, the bus that goes down Oakwood
onto Ossington & down down down to Queen Street,
lots of interesting new shops on both sides, Babel, for example,
that was before your time, you silly twit, you probably took it
last week.

The Truth

They hate us — those starchy fiction readers —
because we write poems about ideas
& perspectives.
            I tell Mrs. Shalowski this as I meet her
coming home from the supermarket.
                        "You should write poems about
young girls," she tells me. "I know," she says,

lifting her dark head with its thick curly hair proudly,
"people like that sort of thing."

"I liked your poem about Einstein," she says,
"because it told me how stupid he really was in his life,

but ideas and perspectives," she says, "hah, I don't know."

And I notice — standing there in the bright sunshine —
that she's carrying a large pot of geraniums.
"Pink," I say, gesturing at the large pot. "Pink," she says.

"The young girls," I say, "O the young girls aren't giving me
very much
pink." "Well," she says, "write about it. Tell them that life
without sex
stinks." And off she goes with her large pot of pink
geraniums — a total enemy of literature,
but a great defender of the truth.

Life Enthusiasts

I was thinking of you this morning
& of a new word which means "terracotta, apricot and blue"
just the sort of word that might be useful
if you were to break up your present marriage & start dating
an archaeologist.
You
speaking of archaeology, as I was, back in the apricot light
 of 1970 to '74,

                    you had — & I hope you still have —
such an immense talent for enthusiasm, so fluid, ebullient
not to mention how beautiful you are in the photos we took
the night we were making God's Eyes, blue & red yarn,
or —
One of the most amazing things about the human mind
is our capacity for changing our values
sometimes on a thin dime. Initially, I was crazy about you
but I thought your interests were sort of tame, not lame,
not a game, just a bit tame: geography, & seed distibution,
& what is nature, or the evening you were off to see a print
of "Wild Strawberries" & I was off to one of my anti-war meetings.
Well of course we change, & we change all over the place.
I remember your father's name was Henry & he was born in
Strasbourg, the family business was on Eglinton,
you put a major emphasis on Flaubert for some reason, so do I,
the real me, I still have the 1914 French fireman's helmet
you gave me for one of those birthdays
somewhere in between 1970
& 1974.

Breaking Up with Miriam Mulstein

I remember the Sunday afternoon she told me
over the phone that it was all off,

                                    or it was sort of
off, or something. I was living at 66 Harvard

north of Queen, just off Roncesvalles. A big ground floor.
I walked up & down the hallway smoking foolish cigarettes
for about 2 hours. It was probably comic. I'm sure it was comic.

Because, just like they say in movies, time passes.
Ingrid Bergman leaves Humphrey Bogart at the airport in *Casablanca*.
Of course she leaves.
Of course she loves him. She thinks he's great. She's not mad
about anything.
                      But if she doesn't leave him
then what the hell will they make a film about? Desert birds
or peach sorbet à la that little French café in Tangier?
We remain friends. Of course I miss her like crazy.
We correspond. Hello new experiences.

Platforms

So, I fell in love with the smile of this girl
called Natalya
from Peterborough, she likes Toronto, she's studying acting,

we flirted all over the place like a couple doing a tango,
she was talking to me about Einstein & stratospheric clouds
while she ran off 10 slices of seasoned turkey breast

& I was talking about the dynamics of the contemporary novel
an example of which, a stunning example,
I am in the process of completing & I think it's majestic.

But something moved the steering wheel to the left instead of the right,
I wound up on the soft shoulder of the interactive dynamic
which has happened to me before, let me tell you, mister,

she's dating a good-looking young guy in an electric wheelchair
he's a blues fan & O I don't know what else
& they smoke a little dope & have sex & talk about life

& drink tequila with slices of fresh lime.

"You're a conceited fathead," she tells me, "you're a jerk
who doesn't respect how hard other people have to work to survive."
"Not true," I said, look, mister, I told her, but good,

but she wasn't listening. She likes the guy, she feels comfortable.
Who am I to squawk about other people's decisions.

But let me tell you, we all have to struggle against something;

I don't punch an alarm clock in the morning but I have to struggle
against depression, I have to struggle against invisible fears,

I have to work for 2 years to produce a book & who's listening?
"Well," she said, "you're a sucker," she said. "What else is new?"

Poems I've Thought of Writing

a poem about a great bear
a poem about the Golden Gate Bridge in San Francisco
does it really have a golden gate
of course not, but it's the bridge John Berryman jumped off
a poem about how beautiful & talented & vulnerable Laura Nyro was
a poem about my old life before April 12
O April 12
a Thursday
a Thursday in the great genesis flood of days of 2001
even a simple oat cake with sweet butter
& a slowly peeled juicy navel orange seem different now
a poem about why I don't speak to Michael Ondaatje anymore
well, for one thing I never bump into him at Bar Mercurio
a poem about generosity
a poem about why I liked Dos Passos so much when I was 21
a poem about Jeanne Moreau doing her imitation of a train
pulling out of a station in Truffaut's *Jules et Jim*

You can see at a glance how spread out I am between nostalgia
& whole wheat bread & love & secular days

a poem about Raquel Welch in that leopard Danskin
       with the men's Olympic Swim Team standing around her all in the nude

Your Effulgence Disorients Me

There are approx. 52,846 different things
in the wide blue world
                & here are 11 of them:
John Coltrane's playing on *Giant Steps* distracts me
from my thoughts about the falling dollar; but at
the same time it gives me a self-enclosed focus;
nicotine, absurd, ridiculous;
a fresh orange chilled under cool water split in half;
a copy of Ian McEwan's *Amsterdam* makes me want to go there;
Matisse is displaced in my head for a few moments
by Egon Schiele's *Adele Harms in gestreiften Kleid*, 1917,
the design of the dress is sort of amazing;
a large photo of a contemporary retro 1920s corset
by a Toronto designer; bananas; if I have chicken for supper
it won't be chicken with almonds and pistachios
& basmati rice; a hardcover guide to Italian verbs;
several promises made to me last week by a very pretty
Registered Massage Therapist, I will get better, the left hip;
it's so sunny, a remarkable afternoon, I don't think
I want to see a film tonight, *A Time for Drunken Horses*,
I still haven't seen that one & now of course it's gone.

Sometimes I get a headful of rose petals & cayenne & notes
from other lives & other periods, better than now? Different.
The problem with your effulgence is that it comes in a binary form,
too wet, so to speak, or way too, shall we say, uh,   dry.

Adele Harms on the other hand is always Adele Harms,
a glorious riot of repression & emotion & colour,
but of course untouchable, someone I've never actually met.

Facing the Streetcars

Let's face it, the world is rocketing past me.
Like one of those bacon & cream-coloured Queen streetcars
racing west or east to Neville Park at 60 MPH
or so it seems.
I think therefore I am.

We have to concentrate on one thing at a time.
I often let the diversity of the Adele Harms distract me.
And passion. A lion called passion. Passionate relationships distract me.
O passion & breakups can totally blur & confuse me.

I would be better I think as a museum guard at the AGO,
someone about 50 with a well-trimmed beard.
"Could you just step back, O, maybe a yard?
The museum would like you to give the Picasso an extra yard."
This big blue & brown Picasso from 1946 is on loan
from the Art Gallery of Marseille. It's on loan
as our bodies are on loan. Forever. An effulgent word.
I would be better perhaps as a handler or colour commentator
for some of these major art exhibits, a young reviewer perhaps
with a nice tweed jacket & clipboard of notes, go ahead
bump into me down at the Power Plant or coming up from the street
into a small champagne-splashed crowd at the Redhead Gallery,

go ahead, see how my axiom works: not burdened at all by the busy
affairs of the ego, but empowered at all times by the simple
technology in my hands. A recent journal page says *empowered* is
not only as resonant as malt but a very clear word. O a better word.
Chick Correa, genius, *ne plus ultra*, genius hands.
Return to Forever, hands, hands, what else

could they call this large blue & brown 6 x 5 Madonna?
Who cares what kind of jacket I'm wearing?
Return to childhood, perhaps.
How about return to ground . . . ?

Drunken Horses

I still haven't seen *Drunken Horses*, and now it's gone.
Naturally. Everything passes, even as we walk down Yonge
to get in on the opening night of this little Waldorf Café on Charles,
something is always passing, something is being lost,
but the seared scallops with a mustard mayo were good, some
satisfaction. Did Otis Redding write "Satisfaction"? I think
Mick & horse-faced Keith Richards wrote it way back in the late '60s sitting
out on the front steps of the American Hotel in Barcelona
waiting for the roadies & the gear & the equipment van.
The desire to keep up with everything
I fall in love with everything, I bounce,
I've got india rubber balls, I don't look like Fred Astaire,
not really, not this morning, but it's summer & you're ready to go.
We need some chicken Café Brussel & a bottle of cheap Georges Duboeuf.
This sounds totally doable. Baby, I can get my head around you.
Baby, sweet potato, I can get my head around you.

Scarlett Johansson

Scarlett Johansson at 32, or at least I think she's 32,
on the cover of *Harper's Bazaar*, January 2009,
she's soooooo goodlooking
I don't usually flip through magazines while I'm shopping
but I couldn't resist — flip flip flip, Dolce & Gabbana ads,
DKNY, Klein, what what no Oscar de la Renta no William Beene
& bang hands up partner here she is on page 74 — a large
head & shoulders lovely face bright scarlet evening dress,
very
shall we say
very formal;
next page, full figure, well yes, she has a great figure,
same full-length evening dress, same lovely shade of red
not a whiter shade of pink, was that Procol Harum, I guess so,
I'm not a voyeur, I don't look in people's wndows
although I suppose a lot of magazines are windows or a window in a sense,
I should have read the text, somebody probably got 2500 for writing it,
but I was in a rush, I'm always in a rush, Jennifer Aniston, same month,
freezing cold in New York, Chicago & Toronto, posed in the nude
for a different magazine, I guess it all depends
on who you're friends with at the time.

Watermelon Summer

     I suppose I'd like to think of summer
& southwestern Ontario
                       or more north around Gravenhurst or Bracebridge
chunks of main highway & lots of concession roads
back roads township roads rural route 1 or RR #2

& think of water, lakes, lots of lakes,

but I don't I think of watermelon & ice cream & outdoor burgers.

Then walk down to the water & smoke one forbidden cigarette,
put it out on some stones,
                     sitting there beside the water,
& talk to you one more time, one last time, you heartbreaker

in a red dress, no, not really, you heartbreaker in rip-off denim

shorts & a pale brown t-shirt that says "Corporate Success

for the Fun of It." Well, now, hearty ha ha, haha.

Poetry Reading, Oak Park, Ill.

His name is Eric,
                he's about 17
& has what appears to be a line of white salt about his eyebrow.
"So,"
      he says, "if you're a great poet,
how come you haven't written any big poems like *Maximus*

or invented
          something?" I tell Eric that all my poems

are about 2 pages long, & they're all great. "Where did you
buy the jeans?" I ask him,
               "Are they Wranglers?"

He says, "Yes, they're Wranglers." "I never wear Wranglers," I tell him,
"Levi's, sometimes,
         & GAP."   "O," he says, "You're an older guy,"
he says, "you
         shouldn't wear jeans at all." He looks awkward. His
girlfriend is leaning over his arm showing off 2 perfect pears

casually covered up with a cardigan.   "2 pages," I tell her,

"so you can see some kind of resolve
               without reading for an hour."
An hour is a long time, that could be a drive to the edge of town
for a hamburger.

Behold the Lillies of the Field

    Seamus Heaney *not*
exactly
        the greatest Irish writer I've ever read
got
the Nobel Award last year for his general achievement
in such books as *Signals*.
                He's a pleasant mild-mannered
Irishman
born in the north, I believe, in Belfast
called Ulster by the Protestants
& of course there are 2 wildly different lobbies
one says a true Irishman is good-natured & a hell of a drunk
& by the Lord Jesus he has to be a Catholic
but of course he never goes to Church
they only go to Church in the pubs — publican publican can you be
hoisting or toasting me another pint of the common plain over here?
The other lobby is obviously smaller
since it's entirely in the north but it would include people
like Brian Friel who is one hell of a playwright for suuuure.

Awards are getting commoner & commoner.
Everybody wants to jump into the act & wave their fist around.
It's getting just a little teensy weensy bit ridiculous.
Did James Joyce ever win the Nobel Award?
No, no he didn't. Did Henry Miller ever win the Nobel?
You've got to be joking, Harry. Did D.H. Lawrence ever win the Booker?
Let's say for a gorgeous book like *Women in Love*.
O well, different time period, different customs.

But in general I don't think literary critics can afford to
get involved in discussing every award winner that turns up.
Renata Adler, for example, didn't she win a National Book Award?
Whereas Wm. Gaddis & John Barth, I don't think they've ever won an
award for any of their novels. They're not couch potato writers.
Or, on the other hand, how do you know they're any good?

Remember Sean?

God,

　　　Sean Penn — remember him — Sean
must be almost 40

　　　　by now — & all the publicity about the slap
he gave Madonna at a public reception? Just water under
the Williamsburg Bridge.

　　　　　　I don't believe he actually did slap
Madonna. I think Sean just brought his hand up about several
inches away from her ear & said

　　　　　　　"O when are you going to stop
acting like America's #1 golden blonde rosy-cheeked
virgin

　　bimbo? For Christ's sake, you're almost 30. Put some
clothes on, at least put a pair of jeans on over those black
lace panties & that ridiculous garter belt,

　　　　　　　　you

look
terrible." And the *New York Times* manufactured the whole
event as,

　　Sean slaps Madonna.

In/Out

At G's (the small Tibetan variety cum
grocery mart I go to in the mornings down on Bloor Street)

(& believe me
this is a family cum super or grocery mart
with an astonishing older woman
who looks very imperious in a black sweater
& med expensive slacks & can still bend over & touch her toes
& does not believe that China should control Tibet;
& an enterprising son
& a rather lovely exquisite daughter-in-law
& the sister of the son
who taught me to say Burrh Rensa
which is the only Tibetan I speak & which means Free Tibet)

Anyway,
        carrying my dozen eggs & a copy of the Saturday
Globe and Mail in which I will surely find
as sure as God made little chickens & they made eggs
some lavish theatre reviews & bits & pieces & snippets
to do with entertainment all over America,

I notice for the first time in leaving that there is a white
card on the front door with OUT
in large black letters
(because there was a confusion with the other front door
which is locked, naturally)

& someone has written in large ballpoint YORGOS

which is Greek for OUT.

Titles

            Wetlands is a good title — it doesn't give
too much away
            but it hangs there — bright orange on the pale
brown cover — as clean and precise as a coloured spinner
for brook trout. You have to be careful with titles. You've
got other people besides readers and graduate students
to worry about. You've got the café graduate students.
They like to analyze titles, and of course there may be a bit
of that in almost everybody.
                Flaubert's Parrot for example,
that's a pretty stupid title. We don't think of Flaubert
as having a parrot; Flaubert had *Madame Bovary*
and that's what we want to see. *U.S.A.* by Dos Passos
sounds more like a travel guide than a novel, but it is
a good book.
            The idea is to create an interesting patch
of attention-getting colour on the cover, but the café graduate
students don't understand this, they think this is the novel,
and they sit outside in the bright sunshine and debate it
for hours. *Nana*, by Zola, that's a good title,
                       or *The Blue Hotel*
by Stephen Crane. But *Brightness Falls* by Jay McInerney,
what does it mean? Brightness doesn't fall, darkness falls,
brightness rises. Think of the jokes about the title *The Grapes
of Wrath*. But it got people to open the book. The café graduate
students are too smart to open the books. They study the covers,
and then they go to the café and order cappuccino w/ a double
Hennessey's on the side and talk about gossip
in the abstract.

It's Lonely at the Top

It's lonely at the top   if you want to
get to the top of rock & roll. For example:
the beautiful slim young dark-haired girl
who encourages you for weeks, wet sheets, Jack Daniel's,
& then you wake up one morning & nothing's gone
but the two songs you've been developing for months
are out on a California singles label with your girl's name.
You don't even get a credit line as a good bassist.
Or the standard urban myth you've already heard about —
the producer who sets you up with a contract & a label,
everything you've wanted now the dark-haired girl is
swimming in the Pacific just off Venice Beach,
& only after you've cranked out a whole brilliant album
do you realize that your contract is going to penalize
you, the artist, songwriter, etc. if you sell less than 25,000.
It's lonely at the top of rock & roll, they've all been there,
Coltrane, Oscar Pettiford, Amelia Curran, Patricia O'Callaghan, Jenny Lewis,
Bowie, Lou Reed, Jagger, you wonder how on earth a sweet girl
like PJ Harvey ever survived. I don't know. It's lonely
at the top if you're talented & you want to rock & roll until after dark.

A Comic Moment Toward the End
of a Serious Relationship

I remember you walking around naked
early morning
                    nothing on but a blue t-shirt.

I was sitting at the kitchen table with my coffee.

You came into the kitchen & threw open the fridge door,
I'm not sure,
                    my darling, if I would say
melodramatically,
                    & you leaned over
with your lovely dark head down around the middle shelf.

I thought, who knows, what a lovely ass, so plump & shapely,
isn't it too bad that we're into a serious breakup,

there is nothing to salvage at this point,
no manoeuvre that could possibly get the car straightened out.

Suddenly you turned around, spun around, maybe, whirled.
Are you looking at my cunt?

And I said, well now, you're facing me. It's about time.

A Slightly Stoned Descartes

I don't really know the eastern hemisphere of this huge green
planet that I live on.

Names are easy. Names crop up as regularly in my mind as myriads
of wildflowers in a country field. Tunis,

                        Tripoli, Algiers,
for example, I remember those names from high school
& of course they're exotic.

Luxor is the Egyptian city close to El Alamein — the Valley of
the Kings. We've all seen — photographs — of the gold sarcophagus
of Tutankhamun,

         the boy King of Egypt who died in his 20s.

But what does it all mean? I don't know that Nietzsche was insane
when he died,

         he was possibly insane on & off,
Who knows why Virginia Woolf committed suicide?
Was Malcolm Lowry *de facto* a Canadian novelist?
Here I am alone with
a small Globe in my hand
& then you get sloppy records & bad biography.

Bright Red Numbers on a Digital Morning Clock

October dark. Nothing wrong with it, I love the dark
sometimes, I'd love to be in the dark with you right now, cute bunny,
but what is *it* doing here so early, too early for September 7
morning 6:35 red red, red & yellow, is that what the clock
says?

Grants

　　　　Now that the fabulous strawberry jam on
golden
　　　　Dimpflmeier rye toast grant application
has been rejected
　　　　There is no mail *no* mail to look forward
to. Poor boy,
　　　　poor boy you're gonna hang.

Lateral Interference in Daily Life

"Hello, hello, you look terrific, you're so slim,"
says my friend Sarah checking me out & smiling widely.
Forgive me for breathing
is there something I didn't notice
I haven't been on a diet.
Sam tells me I look older when I run into him down on College St.
Well, I look older with a beard.
A fraction.
A decimal point.
Maybe it's the difference between boys and girls.

My luck to drink Jack Daniel's, my luck to drink milk.

I used to have a girlfriend who complained
Why do you always wear blue jeans, people think you're a hippie,

O my gawd, a hippie, well give me that zilch bag & light my fire,
I've got a girl with a voice that sounds like an angelic choir,
different girl,
different choir,

I used to have a girlfriend whose name was Jean
she was doing her Ph.D. in childless couples & she loved me, she wasn't mean,
she was sweet
O she was sweet as tupelo honey,
come on, this is a wonderful night for a moondance
& baby I want to do a moondance with you,
my luck to eat pasta fagioli my luck to eat vichyssoise,
grab it by the ears like the White Rabbit & see what time it is.
Oh yeah, this young kid says to me down at This Ain't a Blues Bar,

"I've seen your name around. You published a couple of books
in the '70s." Uneducated little zombie.
I've published a dozen books since then
& won a number of awards & influenced some famous people.

My luck to go to Gravenhurst, my luck to go to Mexico.
Be polite, laugh, don't get upset about the world news.
Check these new poems, it's 2007, they're fabulous.

I'm Not Walking in Circles

Who's that girl on the cover of *W*?
camisoles aren't trendy anymore. Eggplant is trendy,
is delicious with a little marinade
with a little bit of luck
I think eggplant was the tofu of the 1960s, so,

hot head
bitter lemons
skylights
tomatoes
subways   well, nothing's for sure
I've got a mouthful of tinned pears
pear absolut
sheer pellucid loveliness let loose upon our senses
in the tumult of this wild May
pistachios, O for the love of God, just give me a small bag of
chocolate
the stories go round & round. Julia Roberts talks about
growing up. I'm with you in Taos, N.M., Julia, I grew up
a long time ago & then
                    I changed. Let's say I went clear. I'm not grown up anymore.
The only striking aspect of Edmund White's *Nocturnes for the King of Naples*
is the cover. The cover is very good indeed.
Sherri Saunders was at Trattoria Giancarlo last night. I split
a house in Lennoxville, with her ex-husband. A nice guy,
athletic, he's in the English Department at Bishop's,
skis very well but he's crazy about Derrida & Lacan. Lacan?
Derrida? This isn't 1961.
Hot head. Nobody sends a blue flare up unless they're in trouble.

Stories.

The story of our lives.

We were the champions of our class. Some people think I'm crazy
but they don't know me at all. We were heroes — yeah yeah yeah.

I weep like Adonais for the lost time of 2004.

Don't be gloomy. Now it's 2006.

It only takes a small amount of time

to do something totally unique.

Go to India, write *Twilight of the Idols*.

Life is good.

Who was that girl on the cover of *W*?

God I don't know.

I haven't seen a copy of *W* for years.

She Thinks Zen Is Too Intellectual

It's a hot Thursday afternoon & I'm hanging out
with my friend Paul Fieldstone at a little café
called Dooney's on Bloor St.   I'm talking about this girl
I've just met,
          Jenna, young, maybe 26, she's a receptionist
for a dentist I see once or twice a year, you know,

dental hygiene, cleaning, whitening, stuff like that.

I say, she's got the most peaceful face I've ever seen.
Very centred, she's not distracted by anything. If I say,
how long do you think Gloria is going to be?
she just laughs very peacefully and says O not a long time.

Paul shrugs & says, "You're not telling me anything. What does
she look like?" He makes that egregious hourglass motion
with his hands that women tend to dislike.

I say, O yeah, she's all there, beautiful face, lovely body.
But it's this peacefulness that gets me, she stops me cold.
I just sit there & smile at her like a dumb puppy.

I don't know how people like Jenna do it, I say, one thing,
they're totally not involved in issues,

& if a relationship gets steamy, a problem, they automatically
define it as a bad relationship, they call it bad karma. I laugh.
Paul says, "Well there you go, skychief, she's got a simple belief
system, & probably thinks you're adventurous & all mixed up."

Ibid.

No I'm not I'm not a pedant
but I am crazy about information
& I store a lot of information

& I correct you sometimes about things like early Jean-Luc Godard
films
& you get annoyed
                              Well, there you go

But no I'm not a pedant, definitely, no, I'm not, I'm amiable
Self-assured? maybe,
but easygoing, pleasant, fun to be with —
you should invite me for a pleasant supper
I do fabulous grilled lobster
                              You make the salad, okay?

People will stop calling me a pedant when I stop taking
myself so seriously & I start laughing
                              right in the middle

of saying No, Jean-Luc Godard did not direct
The Mother and the Whore, The Mother and the Whore
is a brilliant film b&w ab. 3hrs.
by Jean
Eustache — and you can see Eustache playing himself
on the train in Wim Wenders' *The American Friend.*
So good, so fun.

Wills

No,
                    I don't have a 6-year-old called Harriet
daughter with curly red hair
& a gap between her front teeth. So,
                    who the fuck
do you think
I'm supposed to leave all my money to? The 4-bedroom

house in Willowdale
lots of nice willow trees on some of the streets
the Mercedes-Benz,
                    banana yellow, 4-door, sedan model,
the big summer cottage, I think the one in Gravenhurst
with the wrap-around outside porch
screened for summer evenings. Don't you understand
that — now that I've had my say —

I don't really have anything. Just my health
& a few personal possessions — a filing system etc. —

& 11 published books that haven't sold very well.

On Getting Over a Depression

Laughter is the best, it's that simple,
don't go to a psychologist.
You'll spend an hour x 40 appointments talking about
your childhood.
Laughter.
Laugh a lot. Start off doing it by yourself
& then admit
the great confession
the really great confession
that you need people, others, interesting colourful people.
The girl beside me
is laughing her head off, almost literally, à la the headbangers,
there are six of us & we're at Clinton's on Bloor South,
we have jug beer
which is good because it lasts longer than wine
& you don't get drunk too quickly
getting drunk is also a good way of getting over a depression
but this poem is all about laughter.
That Robin Williams is so funny, the girl on my other side says,
I thought I'd piss myself, I think I did, he drives me crazy.
Bergson's theory of laughter is too superficial
Meredith's theory of comedy is too Abbot & Costello slapstick
you need those other faces around the table gulping beer & laughing.

I woke up the next morning & felt wonderful, relaxed, light,
although I can't remember a single thing I learned, my friend,
except that laughter is profound.

Book City on a Saturday Morning

Is it a writer's hangout? Not that I know of, not really,
not a hangout. I'm always surprised by the variety of people
I never seem to have seen before.
                                        I do the book tables on
the ground floor, tag up with various books I could probably
take out of the library & read at home, Zadie Smith's *White Teeth*,
good book, Martin Amis' *The Information*, James Frey's *A Million
Little Pieces*, the book with which he was a big sensation
— look, it's a terrific book — on the *Oprah Winfrey Show*,
& then when someone blew the whistle, a whistleblower blew
the whistle, & claimed Frey had never been in jail etc.,
Oprah was forced to more or less distance her lovely self,
We bear Mr. Frey no ill will, she said, in the sound clip I heard.

I met Alice Parsons at Book City, a lovely Indo Canadian girl
in her 20s who almost immediately as soon as we began talking
told me that she was in love & happy. Plus it's great May
weather, I said. We talked, we dated, just a couple of times,
we talked about a lot of books. Or Fern Eckler — it turned
out that Fern & I had a few friends in common. We talked,
we saw each other for coffee a couple of times, Dooney's,
certainly convenient & they've got great chocolate cake.
She was married, so, so what, we talked about a lot of books.
A number of writers who live in the Annex area use Book City
but I wouldn't say it's a writers' hangout, good store
lots of people, lots of books.

Neu Gedichte

"There are so many new restaurants in Toronto these days,"
she said —
this is Marjorie, whom you haven't met before.

"Well," I said, "Bar-salon cum bistros,
& classic bistros like Peter Pan."

"It's challenging," folding her napkin, "all those luxe luxe places."

Sure, I said, we don't really need any more ' ' ' ' quotes,
the new is all around us,
the lambs of summer are all around us,
Toronto is the most gullible city in America, look, I'm not
saying it isn't also one of the 2 or 3 most terrific

there are probably some new faces at Serra tonight, so what?
I enjoyed the seafood chowder at the Gladstone with pretty April
but I had to go back to the kitchen with my wide bowl & say,

"more broth for God's sake, more baguette, how about some fucking butter?"

& even then we simply uncovered the bare facts about the salmon chunk,

I could do just as well with a 7 oz. tin of Goldstar or Clover Leaf,
imagine how much fun it would be if we could make the scene in
Winnipeg the first time Groucho Marx was at the Biltmore & he met Danny Kaye
the first time I heard Odetta, who passed recently, a few days ago,
the first time I heard Bruce Springsteen & he was really new or neu whichever,
the first time I heard Ray Charles sing that classic "Making Whoopee,"

"O," she says, "you're over 40," & I say, "you're right, I've got a large mind, I don't think M.G. Vassanji is the new Camus, I don't think Jack White is the new Little Richard."

People Who Make the Scene

The poet from Scranton, P.A., who comes on stage with
the camel,
Eric Bogosian, because he never stops talking, and then he
does interviews about how he *can't* stop talking; well, that's
interesting,
Beverly Peele, the gorgeous black supermodel, has just
become the first black model to have a mannequin cast in her likeness,
it's gorgeous also, and slightly taller than she is, but
that's life;
Paul Taylor has just composed his 100th dance, I guess this is a
serious achievement, it's called "Spindrift," a nice name, and it's
for 1 male soloist and 11 other dancers. Taylor's from Miss. originally,
like Capote,
like Jasper Johns, they all came north around the same
time. People who like to make the scene.

Millions of books are sold every year, but I think a lot of people
just buy them, glance at the first few pages and then file them on the
living room coffee table, that's what living room coffee tables are
for, unless it's something really important, like *Hamlet* on CBC radio,
that was good.
Or *Law & Order*. All kinds of people
collapsed in front of the television set every night to watch *Law & Order*.

Of course there are people who actually read, and who listen to
text. I like reading. I like the flow of type. I have to admit I'm
biased. But I'm grounded. It's a good
clear stance.

How to Become a Better Person

Get up every morning at 6:45.
Drink 6–10 glasses of water every day.
Avoid Evian it's everywhere it's too damn popular.
Try to achieve regular work habits.
Don't skip.
Don't do hopscotch.
Stay out of dark restaurants.
Make filing a fairly spontaneous pastime not a ritual avoidance.
Avoid people who immediately begin their first sentence with "I."
Don't be taken in by avant-garde films.
Give up those pathetic attempts to keep up with new ephemeral novels.
Tell people, Look, it's either Proust or *Vanity Fair*, fuck the rest.
Never believe that any magazine can offer you 364 new ideas on style
or how to get along with women when they're in a bad mood.
Give up on diets. Skip supper. Go to a movie.
Don't give up on chocolate, junk food, pizza or rare red roast
beef sandwiches with a single slice or perfectly fried eggplant
& a big wallop of fresh, juicy tomatoes.
Say a mantra every morning when you wake up.
Don't believe more than 2½% of the stories people tell at launches,
they fake hot stories at the drop of a hat.
Don't buy a dachshund. They hate being left alone during the day.
Take more interest in the eastern hemisphere — read up on the history
of India, buy calendars of exotic rainforest frogs, study Bangkok.
See your first Sam Peckinpah film. Go retro.
Dump your Norah Jones CDs, buy some Fat Boy Slim.
None of us are going to live forever, not even David Bowie.
Don't switch to IBM. Stay with Mac. Wear a suit once in a while.
Go out with older women. Nothing is going to save your life except
more contemplation & better work, study Frank Sinatra's ballads.

Sinatra & Juliette Greco.
Ok, it's a guilty pleasure, like chocolate.
Go out for breakfast. Go big time
on mantras & impulse signals.

What constitutes a great impulse signal?
Be natural, well, be yourself.

Dismissiveness

The Universe is everything. But it overwhelms me.
I can't compete.
I can't rise up.
Let's think about this proposition.
I had 2 slices of ham & a wedge of lemon & raspberry
cheesecake for breakfast an hour ago.
The Universe is nothing.

Are Most of Us a Little Crazy?

The young girl with orange hair & a large steel lip ring.
The 65-year-old professor in a grey tweed suit who talks to himself.
Good-looking 41-year-old poets who return to *Treasure Island*.
The large curly-haired blonde woman with two shopping bags on the subway.
Bill Clinton because she probably wasn't a good lay anyway.
Howard Stern because he *obviously* does too much coke.
Anybody who criticizes Rainer Fassbinder without seeing *Mother Kurster*.
All university professors who dislike Thos. Pynchon's *Mason & Dixon*.
A young Chinese guy with a brush cut giggling to himself over a copy of *Esquire*
    or *Wired* magazine.
People who delay the elevator on humid 86-degree days.
Casually dressed men carrying unusually large attaché cases.
Women with short hair who have bizarre recovered memories.
The gorgeous young Japanese assistant chef at *Segovia* restaurant.
Michel Foucault for writing a really marvellous book about the history of insanity.
Neil Young for writing I want to see you dance again.
I think Michel Foucault would love some of
these people. Or would he? Foucault was an academic.
People who go crazy about banana splits.
Ezra Pound, well, you know, he looks sort of crazy.
Lee Bailey on roller-skates w/gym shorts crossing the kitchen at *China Blues*.
Garth Drabinsky for being just a little heavy-handed.
All married women who go to Freudian analysts.
T.S. Eliot for not hiring Dylan Thomas to read *The Waste Land* for him.
All married men who go to late Jungian analysts.

Galileo for proving what we knew all along — we are less important than the sun.

10 Reasons Not to Buy a Smart Car

Don't buy a smart car if you are a musician & you play
upright double bass like the great Oscar Pettiford. It won't fit
in the car. A great car, a novel idea, not a gas guzzler, smart
it parks like a dream.

Not a great car to take out on the big
highways of America if you decide to drive to L.A. Remember
Jack & Neal from the hippie days? They had a regulation Chev
V6. Of course we can always do better. Get a driveaway Ford
& go to L.A. or S.F. Don't buy a smart car if you have a sexy
girlfriend & no place to make love. She has a roommate
you have a roommate. Go to Avis. Rent a big 2006 Ford. You'll
have lots of fun. What about carpool participation? Only
if you're a high school student. Grade 12 basketball players
are tall but they're flexible. No, no you can't take a big
shaggy St. Bernard out to the special vet in Mississauga in a
smart car, it won't work, the dog will be unhappy, the police
will bust you because of the dog's head pointing out the window
& wailing very mournfully in Swiss French. A floating card
game? This has been done on the 401 but not in a smart car,
go ahead try it, you can be the first, you'll get busted
plus you won't get your straight flush across the net. Most
drivers find the smart car a bit light & inadequate on the 401
or the Gardiner in general, those big big 4-door cars beat
past you like a tirade, plus a Lexus plus a fast Mazda. *Not.*
Skiers beware, you'll have to put the skis out the window.
Great for tennis players. Everybody should buy a smart car
& drive all over the place in the city.

How to Save Your Life

Stop eating rare roast beef
Go for long walks in the morning before breakfast
Spend twice as long in the shower & use a loofah
Don't spend any time on pointless exasperation
Go to at least one movie a week
Go to see a Henry Jaglom movie
Don't take the daily headlines seriously
the Canadian dollar will stop falling if they fire Chrétien
Fall in love & tell yourself it isn't forever
Start re-reading Proust but read slowly, take a long time
Go to see a Jim Jarmusch movie
Express yourself   admit you don't
really think Smashing Pumpkins are always all that good
Nobody is as good as Dizzy Gillespie was when you were 21
Obviously
Nobody is as good as Roy Orbison was when you were 15
How do you pronounce notorious? Isn't it really noto-rious?
Do not give up eating rare roast beef
Give up smoking
Give it up at once   that's the only way
it's a ridiculous   & silly habit
Write every morning   even if you're busy as blazes
I love that expression   busy as blazes

Reach orgasm every night by whatever means seem reasonable
Reach orgasm sounds geographic
Can you imagine, Reach, Orgasm, Pennsylvania?
Forgive people who aren't important anyway
They know not what they haven't managed to achieve
Give 100 dollars to the YMCA
Go, go for whatever it is it isn't death

Go swimming once a week

Dizzy

I think of Gillespie's cheeks
which are enormous
                              & of his swivel trumpet pointed skywards,
& I suppose
vaguely   that he has enormous hands.   This is how
we create stereotypes in America out of perfectly valid
material.
Photographs, after all, are valid, aren't they?

      The fact is that he may have liked underdone pork chops
with red peppers & a touch of hot sauce
will probably strike a young New York reviewer as irrrr
relevant. Who met him out on the beach in Fla.
or who met him in a bar in Tokyo. He was a Bahai, sort of,
like, he came into the bar one night
& looked at his watch & said, Well, it's sundown,
bring me a woman with long legs and a glass of scotch as big
as my hand. He was good &
                              he was wild. But I don't think
he really was that much better than Art Farmer. He was
different. The African cap is interesting. But it was
those cheeks that made him famous after the photographs
began to appear. He could hold his breath for a long
time. Those cheeks made him appear mythic,
a myth
was being born.

TAKE ME TO THE RIVER

To Die For

"She had one of those to die for dresses on
and she's changed her hair to a sort of post-modern
boy cut."
        — "What sort of shoes did she have?"
"Shoes? I didn't notice. Shoes don't mean anything."
— See Athens and die. Was that Lord Byron? We can
probably look it up. You can look up almost anything,
stars that have gone nova

                        stars that haven't gone nova.
Did Toulouse-Lautrec have any lovers;
who was really big in Claude Monet's life? I'll bet
she had a French name. Toronto has a lot of to die for
lofts these days, 4th story, old factory building,
historic name,
choice location — well, Dufferin & King West, not bad.
Hart Crane's "The Bridge"
not a bridge but, correct, "The Bridge"
turned out to be a to die for poem. If you've got
a nice front porch & your neighbours aren't a problem,
be cool, sit out on
a summer evening, May will do, that's OK,
a glass of cold lemonade with a splash of vodka,
& read pages 24, 25, 26 out loud.
Not loud enough to scare the raccoons,
do wah diddy doo wah. Buddy Holly died in a
plane crash.

Djuna Barnes

Do you remember that girl I told you
about who looked a lot like Djuna
Barnes? She was on the tall side with nicely cut
honey-blonde hair & big loose
sweaters & those comfortable slacks
that are loose but fit around the butt.

She was great. I met her at Chapters
browsing the fiction section
& we had 4 or
5 dates.
OK, it was 4, but she was interesting to talk
to & she was a lot of fun. It turned out she
had a job almost right across the street
at the ROM & she knew some people that I knew
also. She told me that her mother

obviously an interesting woman

had met the famous Walter Kenyon
on many occasions,
Kenyon was somebody I'd read
about, an anthropologist
& a specialist in Huron burial mounds
& the Huron language. Anyway she was a lesbian
& I never did get to see that girl she shared an apt.
with over on Church Street.
I told my barber this story
& he laughed & laughed while he was cutting my hair. It was
a sunny day & they have huge windows in their place

at Av & Dav. "Ha ha," he said, "that's very funny." — Shorter
at the back & up a little bit, I told him. "My sister's
a lesbian," he told me. — No, I said. "Yes," he said. He's
Italian & he was mad as hell about this detail.

Accounting

Cynthia says, "I think God
is an accountant." And I stop in the middle of a
mouthful
                    of veal scallopini & mashed potatoes w/
gravy,
        a large forkful,
                                    there are about 9 of us
counting Peter who designs nifto net sites for people

& several of us — including Cynthia — go to meetings
at this Temple of
                    the Golden Dawn. We have good

people with lots of good thoughts. W.B. Yeats — remember
reading
him in high school? Once out of nature   I shall never
take my bodily form   from any natural thing. Anyway,
yo,
him, Yeats had to give up his membership in TOTGD in 1910
in London
because there were too many crazies coming into the assn. —
Blavatsky,
et others,
les autres. And I said, How can God be an accountant?
That's ridiculous. God
                            has Angels. And the Angels
are supposed to account for everything. "Foolish of me,"
she says,
            she's wearing this wonderful pale lemon loose
shirt & she has crinkly bronze hair, God, she says,

perfect intelligence thinking itself. Yo, I say,
& finish my wonderful scallopini w/ mashed potatoes & gravy
in one long large & healthy gulp.

I Guess Baseball Players Wear Baseball Caps

People who wear running shoes w/out any socks aren't
necessarily sincere.
Uh, no, it ain't necessarily so.
Running shoes,
                    oh, yes,
and that expensive tweed jacket he's got on tonight does
play up the khaki shorts and collarless shirt.

Young poets who turn up at bar reading series
wearing the obligatory double-breasted
black
leather motorcycle
jacket? No, it
doesn't mean they know anything about Pound or Ursula Rucker,
but they probably know something about Nirvana.

ABC

I wonder how Chas. Olson would have changed *The Maximus Poems*
if he had written them in the blue shadow of an ABC special on Mariner.

Marco Polo in China

Marco Polo entered another world in 1260
& left it behind when he returned to Italy

— when the traveller seeking the wealthy port city of Zaiton
leaves Fu-Chau,
               he must cross a river and proceed southeast
for 5 days —

The canals of Venice were still fresh water
Firenze has chapel choirs but no opera house & Milano has no La Scala.

I think of André Malraux & I think of China now & I think of bicycles
— 1000s of bicycles
Every city seems to have stony hills & low market streets.
Millions of bicycles.

Perhaps the future of the world is millions of people
on bicycles. And who will watch us? Obviously not the giant
pandas sitting high up in the comfortable clefts of sweet
bamboo trees.
               He returns to Italy in 1292.
Venice is also a port city. A gateway. The world
O
the
world of the simple ox cart — the world is ⅔ blue water.

Fuses

       I was putting some t-shirts through the laundry
down in the basement the other day

& Geza — the Hungarian super — was working in the repair room
the lights went off.
                  Geza comes out almost immediately.
"Fuse," he says, looking up at the ceiling in the dark —

I can hardly see him — & making adjusting motions with his hands.

So he blew a fuse. I look back at the laundry unit
& my shirts are in full motion swirling back & forth

in the hot soapy water. I close the lid of the white unit
& the lights come on again. Geza's 70, but he's very fast.

I wonder, is it possible that the human mind quite often
does this?

Kansas

We write, drink,

                           eat, have arguments, take

subways & go to work.

            And we all look out from time to time

at California.

         St. John's Nfld, the Electric Boat Co.

& the gorgeous shade of those 2 blue oceans,

                          their flats & swells,

night tones

    their white birds.

Did Blavatsky Ever Meet Edward VII?

Blavatsky   Her middle name was
Petrovna, assumed, she was sort of
amazing.
        Freud didn't really know very much
about the human brain at all,
                the neurology departments
of the 1890s
weren't really that much better than phrenology charts
although they were very big on the idea
of one area
affecting another area — e.g. the nervous system
is continous. Blavatsky,
        an obvious dip head,
a psychic,
photographed by some of the early photographers
c/w her crystal ball
probably knew as much or more about the human brain,
        she looked at all those colourful charts
that were floating around Europe & showed
the Lake of Ambivalence,
        the crown of Desire,
the idea
that the mind is a city & has various arrondissements.
Freud didn't know much.
Blavatsky was a fake, but she didn't dislike sex
& probably knew as much
or more
about the brain. Alexander Graham Bell,
what the hell did you know about the human brain?

O not much, I'd say, not much. But Bell saw that the brain was about 4½"
in height, & that the human ear was rather large,

in fact as large as
a window. So Bell knew a great deal about the human mind, he saw sound.

Legzzz

This isn't gender conscious,
not really,
      & I think sexism means objectionable —

so if I describe you as a leggy girl
that simply means,
      O Daughter of the Gods,
that it would be apt for me to say she's got legs
from here to Canada. That's hip *and* descriptive. You're
tall
      with short, dark hair & one corn braid at the back,
slim,
      expressive, with one of the world's Great Smiles,

& you do have extraordinary legzzz. But, check this, my girl,

we already are in Canada & this is approx. 4,286 miles
of enormous, fertile & diverse American (sic) land.

So, what can I say? How about, she's got legs from here
to Kansas City, Kan. That
                  sounds good. We've never been
to Kansas City & they've got some wonderful music bars.
One suitcase each,
      let's get on the train
& go, & you can put those long legs up on the opposite seat
& we'll talk about life & love all the way to St. Louis.

Fluid Motion

I like the way he simply gives up on a conversation
& moves casually to a different group of people,

no

I'll see you tomorrow, or later, or later gator,

no

little wave of the hand, bird, butterfly or ripple.

It's

rather nice the way he does it as effortlessly as a child
stretching or a dog getting up & trotting out to the porch.

Nothing that would get tangled up in a silly disagreement.

There is a little trick though. He always does it as soon
as the person he's been talking to turns to include or speak
to someone else. It's deft. I've practised it myself
a few times, & done it back to a couple of his squatters. Not sure
if he noticed
or not.

Spreading the Word

It's a clear day
one of those clear sunny days when you can see forever

& who do I see coming down Bathurst Street
but Nadine pushing a large black & yellow wheelbarrow
the kind you can buy at Can Tire for $69.95.

Hello Nadine, hello I call out to her as we approach.

"What on earth do you have in that big wheelbarrow?"
Groceries, some lime cordial, *The Autograph Man*, Zadie Smith.

I wonder about her, an older friend of my girlfriend Susan,
she doesn't have any shoes
okay it's summer
& she's got an old dress that looks straight from the Sally Ann.
I think maybe she is moving
which could read — maybe she's crazy.

"Gossip," she calls out, she doesn't even stop, rude cow,
"fresh shit, night soil, fresh shit."

Boy O boy, I think as she goes past,

I wonder what little café on south Bathurst is buying that treif.

The Nature of Language

I'm sitting in my favourite cafeteria — Master's — eating
a reasonable chicken souvlaki with a Greek salad & rice
& watching the national U.S. youth spelling championship on TV.
I think the age limit is 13 & 14 & they're all fabulously
clean cut & polite with charming mannerisms
& they're largely Midwestern or southern this afternoon at least,
St. Louis, Missouri, someplace in Mississippi, Staten Island,
come on, that's not a state, it's a state of ferry-mindedness.
The rules are that after they're given a word they're allowed
to ask for the etymology, which works well on television,
the young university guy spells it out to them,
they can ask for a repeat, there's some drama or tension here,
they can ask for it to be used in a sentence,

oesophagus, sarsaparilla, tailgate, visceral.
It's fabulous sitting here relaxing on a summer afternoon
watching their seraphic faces — although they never get seraphic —
knotting of fingers, knitting of brows, pursing of mouths,
& then, after taking all the time they can & double checking,
they spell it out,
                    o e soph a gus, there, goddamnit,
that wasn't too bad. My only complaint — & look, I do support
youth & good spelling & I'm not biased against any state
or using an extra s in a word — do they really, confrontationally,
physically, get better sentences? Who knows, it's not hiphop
but it's a totally significant surge in a marvellous language.

Kiev Is Dark at Night and Very Historic.
They Have Warm Lakes to the South.

The lovely young Ukrainian couple
next door
        moved out yesterday. They have both
finished their courses at the university. We used to talk
in the elevator on rainy days and he would point to a pale violet band
intersecting the grey paper towel sky and shrug.
Days when a young horse might go for a long run down Yonge Street.
Days of black coffee at night & scrambled eggs w/ onion for breakfast.

I have no idea where they are moving to. Somewhere.
Perhaps they're moving back to the Ukraine.
Who knows?
We waved goodbye outside as a friend in a windbreaker
helped them load their books & suitcases of clothes into a small Honda.
The girl's name is Olga.
I never did get her husband's last name straight. My fault, no doubt.
Olga is tall and willowy & very pretty with lots of dark hair & big glasses.
How do you say "willowy" in Ukrainian?
Her husband? About medium height & weight, shy, very friendly,
fair complexion, steel rims & a very spare beard.
Perhaps they're on their way,
                        by air, via Paris, via Berlin, who knows,
to some place in the north of Ukraineva.
Someplace like Kiev or Odessa
where a friend of mine spent part of a summer last year.
Peter & Olga.
Peter told me that when he was at university in Moscow
he would go to a little cinema sometimes for about 50¢
& see Russian art films that he had never seen in the Ukraine.

71

Once, somehow or other, he saw *Betty Blue* by Jean Bienix.
There would be cars at night & glasses of vodka.
Do you speak Russian? I asked him.
O sure, he said, I speak some Russian. University Russian,
soup-plate Russian. Goodbye,
                              Peter,
send me a postcard of Kiev at night & tell me what you & Olga
are doing & have you got a job teaching mathematics?
Our worlds are so different but I loved you
even though we never did get to have dinner together.
They put the furniture you couldn't sell out in the side court area.
I couldn't use the extra white bookshelf because I've forced myself
down to a perfect 500 volumes, but that's okay,
I'll put your postcard up on the wall & leave it there
for as long as I stay here.

Unforgettable Men

Woody Allen's a good example,
that face is unforgettable, it's classic schlemiel with a
lot of brooding intelligence, plus, he made *Play It Again,
Sam.*
Glenn Gould sitting at the keyboard
playing *The Goldberg Variations* & humming
to himself over the music is an example.

Richard Gere for the way he played Rick in *Looking For Mister
Goodbar* with Diane Keaton, John Malkovich for his role
as the blind chairmaker in Robby Benton's *Places in the Heart.*
Sam Shepard for his role as Doc in the film version
of Beth Henley's *Crimes of the Heart.*

All those guys with names like
Rick who pose for Calvin Klein ads & have fabulous smiles & gorgeous
bodies.

Some Shocks Are Delicious

When you meet someone & you feel immediate love
a delicious shock of recognition
you look into their face & say, I love your eyes
& your mouth, whatever you've got under those clothes
I want it.

Well-educated Well-read Young Writer Who Can't Finish His First Novel Because He's Obviously Distracted

Women in Love by D. H. Lawrence except that I've never motored across Germany with 2 gorgeous women & a male friend like Gerald.

Moby-Dick by Herman Melville except that I've never been on a major whaling expedition.

Wise Blood by Flannery O'Connor except that I've never known a guy like the itinerant preacher who walks on barbed wire in his bare feet in that novel.

The Sound and the Fury by William Faulkner except that I'm not sure of who to give the role of Benjy to or in what context.

Salt by Herbert Gold except that there obviously has to be another woman.

A Severed Head by Iris Murdoch except that my acceptance of Melanie Klein tends to make it difficult for me to write this novel also.

Jack

What Jack means   when he says,
"You can only talk about what you
can see in front of you" is basically
that Jack can only talk about
what he can see in front of his face.

Cool

Cucumbers are cool
                              it's that pale green shade of
white
I guess that makes them cool
                              not the dark green rind. Pale lemon
gelati is cool
            with or without biscotti
perhaps. Boys & girls. Boy I sure wish

I was cool about you. Men
                        don't make passes
at girls who wear glasses. O sure they do,

I do, & so it's my own fault that I'm broken-hearted.

Traffic

The blue zones of the mind   direct traffic
like a whimsical gendarme in a Paris square. Yonge & Eglinton

has dumped me further south around St. Clair. I can smell spring
in the enormous ravine that runs across the entire city

but is mostly invisible to passing motorists & bicycles.
Now it's dark the bicycles are more distinctive.

Bright young things are eating strawberries & linzer torte
& espresso north of Yorkville. It's dark but only 9:30

on my inexpensive watch. Later, if I turn & look over my shoulder
to the NW, I will see the 10:40 & 10:42 & 10:47 night flights

taking off from Pearson for Los Angeles & Miami.

There's a stirring in the row of trees ½ way across Ramsden Park
where the tiny perfect Mayor used to come home & sail his model

planes up over the trees & of course down on the grass.
Living in Toronto makes us conscious of the continent,

its shifting moods, its peccadillos, its little faults & glories.
I walk slowly now, looking forward to Davenport & Yonge,

espresso, maybe some calamari & a glass of beer at the Pilot.
A dark blue breath of air moves the marble statue of the young

Apollo, a breath of the imagination, I need some espresso for sure,
no perfume & taffeta tonight, how do you stay that young forever?

The 2 Giovannis

I always find it a bit hard to remember the 2 Giovannis
a father & son
who were both principal organists at St. Mark's in Venice
in
      O, you know, 1590
                        & perhaps 1632, reespecktivlee.
So it blows my ever-loving great mind wide open
when a well-intentioned but really fast-paced like the Cisco Kid
program
blurts names out of context or puts J.S. Bach
in Italy on a visit to Corelli that he obviously didn't make.
No, I don't think, uh, that I made that train.
Pronunciations vary almost as much as baseball teams.
A lot of people say concertos, a lot of people say concerti.
What does *molto allegro con fuoco* mean that *fiera* doesn't mean?
History is full of terms.
I love the music, I love thinking about Venice in the 1640s.

I don't know why I get bored with Vivaldi's *The Four Seasons*,
it's all set pieces, it's stock
                     but easy to pronounce.

Free Fall

I pick up on a visual image of racing camels
& take it as far as it goes
                        or perhaps I look at it visually
& see where it goes. It all sounds improbable.

Why couldn't I have thought of something like *The Simpsons*?
I don't think Matt Groening picked this concept out of free fall.
I understand Botticelli's *La Primavera* by direct perception.
I look at it & I know it's a great painting.
The same thing as saying I like it.

The brain looks like a coil of sausages around a number
of specific controls like the medulla oblongata or the pons.
They all have a lot to do with light & with chemical controls.
My dopamines are out of control. Spalding Gray is overlapping Eric
Bogosian. Laurie Anderson isn't in this picture.

Dumb nationalists will look at this & say he's focusing
on U.S. icons; but of course there are about 300 million U.S. citizens
I haven't even mentioned.
How much did the Etruscans influence the course of Italian
history before they were absorbed by new people coming over from Libya?
Carl Gustav Jung would love this morning's example: I put a deadline
on my calendar by circling May 16 & went to the fridge for some
hummus, something to munch on, flatbread, pita, & taking the
black olive hummus out of the fridge it swung in my hand & revealed
a best before date of May 16. I'm easily distracted
            but I'm not immune to karma.

October

Time to pull in, pull down, simplify.
Yes indeed, it's time, ladies & gentlemen,
it's time. Time
              to button the blue & grey tweed overcoat
up to the top
& turn the collar up. Time to stop flirting

& time to concentrate on almost nothing but writing great poems

with those extraordinarily beautiful young waitresses
e.g.
Nicole, Selma,
              the comma is important.

Commas are always important. It's October, 20, 1998, A.D.

Just to be precissssssssse.

Men

"Men are the only other sex there is," she says
flipping the black spaghetti strap from one bare shoulder.
Men are tall and lean and interesting and gorgeous.
Men talk too much and dominate the conversation.
Men are only after one thing   their minds fixed
on the sweet patch of dark between her cool thighs.
Men are rude and bullish about getting their own way.
Men are reflective and kind   good at listening to
problems over a second coffee after dinner.
Men are soft and moony   suckers for a pretty face.
Men are intelligent and erudite but as lost as small boys
in need of someone to make breakfast
and comfort them when they lose at squash.
"Men are violent and crazy," she says,
"my first husband killed a waiter for making a pass."
Men are blessed somehow with explosive passions
and great ideas which win them a place in the world
while women merely stand around and get photographed.
Men are beautiful and have cocks and are lost explorers
of the great fallen cities where they lead grey-eyed camels
and horses and slow mules with a sore front foot.
"Camels," she says, "I've never been interested in camels,
those great humps   those terrifying black mouths . . ."

OBAMA POEMS

George the 3rd Plus His Madness

Okay, my friend, so you're the King of England
or
the Prime Minister of Canada, land of a thousand blue lakes,
or
the Chancellor of Germany or the President of Texas & the 49 states,

that doesn't mean you have to be *in love* with capitalism.

George the 3rd, for example, wasn't in love with the wool mills
that huge industry
an early bulwark along with the new shipping, 3 tall masts & glory, glory,

glory & salt water & flying fish.

George enjoyed putting on a good show, they did it for him,
musicians playing at dinner,
not too many speeches,
some interests in horses, not to mention sports including swordsmanship,

George wasn't in love with capitalism
he was in love with being the King, & a yard of ale with his breakfast,

plus the occasional night time ramble in his nightshirt
talking to the badgers out on the palace's green & fragrant grounds.

The Differences Between Us

There's a songwriting contest on national radio right now,

pick a place in your state that you think calls for a song,
what about
the horse fields in Halifax, a park, a baseball diamond, a ravine,
the caller says
I don't remember ever seeing a horse there but it was a magical place,

another caller thinks the sw corner of Yonge & King
where sits one of the largest & most architectural banks in the world,
but it was on that corner that I first kissed my sweet Daphne Wurtzer.

You get the picture? Of course it's going to go on from Halifax to Victoria,
whatever that is,
                    approximately the same number of miles
as San Francisco to Washington, D.C., where the Potomac meets Atlantic lobster,

or from Philadelphia to Salt Lake City & the mountains of Utah.

You could never do a contest like this. You have too many people.
too many individual states, too many state caps., too many people.

But when I look at movies from the '40s & '50s, I see what we have become,
we have become the America we wanted to be, so cool it, Jack, don't step on it,

And when I listen to songs from the '40s, you know, a nice little bit of Hart,
a gorgeous "It Had To Be You," Gershwin with 2 other writers, *sine qua non*,

I hear the American we have become when we feel like being fanciful
instead of tough.

It takes talent to win a baseball game
but it takes something more to win a contest for national spirit.

Let's give Obama a free train ride from Halifax to Victoria, west of the mtns.,
a simple lunch, boy, he's got a slim waist, some porterhouse for supper.

Obama Campaigning

You have to hand it to Obama
he looks great at all hours of the day
there's no such thing as a one-day stubble
or a rumpled shirtfront

I've never seen him in a t-shirt
he's totally a white shirt & well-chosen tie kind of guy
& that's no lie
you'll have pie in the sky when you die
sure, but that's no lie he's a well-dressed guy

And he speaks well, he's got a great voice,
when he drops down an octave or so to go baritone
he sounds as if he's already running America
God knows, & we know, it's about time somebody did

Where are the social services, where's the new schools money,
whatever happened to health in the promised land?

A young man with a large broom & a good suit
he's going to sweep up Wall St. & keep Texas in its place
It sounds good, it's the only show in town
Who would go to a Lakers game when there's a game like this in town?

But he still hasn't cleaned up Bosch Goldman,
he still hasn't regulated bonuses,
the dollar is soft against the Euro

Pre-emptive Strike

It's remarkably easy to make a cardboard pattern
& then put it down on the sidewalk
somewhere around Bloor & Spadina or Parliament & Carlton

& just paint over it with blue ink, printer's ink, or dye.
3 Jet Fighter planes streaking upward past the viewer:

. . . .

& the words *pre-emptive strike*.

Probably some people feel the Swedish Academy has chosen
Barack Obama
                    because after all, he's a stand-out
& he is the first black President in the history of America.

And after all, who was the first black saxophonist
that word we are now supposed to pronounce sax   oph/onist

so the radio host jokes

in the Tommy Dorsey Band? I have no idea, my mind is a blank.

I think Obama was probably a stand-out way back in high school,
good at defending ideas, a smooth mover defending a friend, *or*

first guy out on the dance floor for the Carole King slow number.

I'm not sure, I think he was in politics by the time he was in college.
I think the Europeans have put him in a discreet circle of people,
no roughnecks,

a line up like Dag Hammarskjöld, Lester Pearson, remember Gorbachev?
I've often wondered if the character in *Stalker*
contains a reference to *Gorby*, that amazing film by Tarkovsky.

Be all this as it may or may not be,
the Head Man of Air Force One has the power to declare a strike
against Tehran or against Korea, both of which would be foolish,

but in actual fact & practice the Head Man sits one end
of a long circle or maybe an oval of top managers
whenever it is, I think it used to be Tuesday afternoon, 2 o'clock,

it's probably changed all the time, plus the meetings are probably longer,

and your job is to prod the head of the CIA & to say things like,

Could the head of the CIA be a little more precise, exact, factual,

or, We keep hearing changeups from State, I'm getting confused.
Use your reasoning powers Barack, we don't want a world war,
we don't want a pre-emptive strike on Tehran.

The Significance of State

I often wonder, as we get more & more technology on the market,
if we could simply replace the Canadian Government
with approx. 50,000 R2D2s
                            & let them bumper & hustle
rubber armloads of papers
back & forth.
                OK. It would be chaos, worse than now.

But take a look at State in Washington D.C. Migawd, Thos. Jeff,
4 enormous buildings —
                     each of them a small city complex unto itself.
Nothing can get final signing because with so many people
there are 1000s of work titles
each one of whom wants to be cut into the cookie   just a crumb or a crumble.
It's slow & laborious. Nixon was obviously unpopular,

otherwise he wouldn't have been so easy to impeach.

Clinton was vastly different & much tougher.

Actually, here in Canada, where I am writing this on a train to Montreal,
I spend every day almost wandering freely
unfettered by a story as to what my country stands for.

I can write the entire Canadian State policy
in one or two sentences on a sheet of paper. Our policy is to support

the aims & endeavours of the U.S., whenever & where it may be
deemed possible & desirable & mutual. Really, you don't need
much more. And if we can open a farm equipment factory in Kenya
okay, good, great; & a large work clothing outlet in Venezuela, okay. Great.

A café in Paris. No, that would be ridiculous. What do you expect

Jean Seberg to come walking in wearing a t-shirt from *Breathless / À bout de souffle?*

TAKE ME TO THE RIVER
PART II

Midwestern, Leaning East to Seaboard

There's something amazing about children in yellow
rainboots. They
                       don't call them "rubber boots," they call them rainboots.
An April day in western Ontario,
                             Binghamton, N.Y., up to Massachusetts
or down to Philadelphia. You see them in groups going on daycare walks,

all those bright shining little faces,

                           their eyes always seem huge,
they want chips, they want a sandwich,
they want to know how much further & exactly where they are going. The GAP

ad with the little black girl (shouldn't we say cocoa at least, black
                      isn't physically accurate) curls tumbling

down both sides of her face,
                    raincoat, & dark hunter green boots. She,
I suppose, is a variable in this poem about Catherine Deneuve & *The Umbrellas
of Cherbourg* come to New York City,
                           or they come to Philadelphia
on a mild rainy day. But who knows? Who knows what happens if we change
her boots to a different colour, or if someone comes in, gives
the young blond boy's wheatsheaf over the forehead a quick trim & they shoot
another picture? Colour is just something we look at, are amazed by
as we are amazed
          by the stars at night

or by flowers by the side of the road as we drive to town or back
again,

& where is the town this time, you shd ask,

                  if you're interested in "geography,"

it's Hancock, in western New York & I think a battle was fought here
during the Civil War. No
                I don't see any yellow rainboots,
an extremely small town with a few stores & not much money, but that's not my

fault,
    is it?

Little Moron

That famous example of Little Moron searching
the pavement on his hands & knees outside the Banco de los
Americos building on Telegraph Avenue in San Francisco
for a 50¢ piece he lost on South Broadway —

        and these 2
guys in Hells Angels jackets stop & watch him. One of them
       says to him,
Little Moron, Little Moron
      what are you looking for? So,
naturally,
        he tells them. And the youngest
of the 2 guys says, So what the fuck are you looking for it in San
Francisco for, d'ya think it rolled all the way to Pennsylvania & all
the way west & down highway 69 and wound up here — outside the
Hispanic bank? And Little Moron says,
       I know what I'm doing,
it's dark on south Broadway at this time of night,
         but here
on glorious Telegraph Avenue with all the golden yellow light
pouring out the front of this roughcast & pink stucco Banco
de los Americos there is an abundance of light. So, he says,
I can see what I am looking for and this is important. They
leave him there on his hands and knees laughing their heads
off; and 2 days later, sure enough, it's amazing, Little
Moron finds a 5-dollar bill, not just any 5-dollar bill,
but an altered 1942 5-dollar bill, a collector's piece. Hallelujah,
says the little sucker, and he proceeds straight through those
black iron grill doors and opens his 57th bank account —
savings, of course. Little Moron is saving up for a piece of
Pennsylvania & he never writes cheques.

Bruce's Yams

You can't get Bruce's Yams for $3.29,
I mean, look, fella
                there's some bulk to this can,
21 fluid oz. 597 ml,
                of course, they're probably disgusting.
Let me take you to the Riviera for delicious whole carrots,
probably a lovely bright orange,
really delicious,
                not too expensive,
Or NO NAME. NO NAME have fabulous med. large tins
of small whole white potatoes,
                CANADA GRADE #1,
for 99¢. It's amazing what they put in cans, Diced Baby Beets
with Harvard Sauce, for example,
                        I have this immediate image
of large numbers of very clean-cut young men in Harvard
letter sweaters
sitting around long tables in the dining room
eating overdone pork roast with large helpings of Harvard Beets.
No,
no, it's not for me. JOLLY GREEN GIANT creamed corn,
that's a bargain
                79¢,
this is a stand out,
but no, I don't think I want JOLLY GREEN GIANT creamed corn.
Then I notice the store has Baxter's
Lobster & Seafood Bisque,
                Bisque de Homard et Poissons de Mer,
on sale for a shocking $1.79.
                        Look, when you stop to compare prices,

this isn't bad. Why don't I buy the Baxter's for $1.79
and
a tin of CANADA GRADE #1 small whole white potatoes,
& just like that,
                    Mr. Jellybuttons,
I've got dinner for 2. 2. Can you believe this?
And if I'm lucky,
                    if you're lucky, fella,
then Sheila just may bring one of those elegant crusty French baguettes,
& possibly a few fresh green beans,
& what else
do we need?

An NFB Full of Luminous Still Photographs

There *are* blue moons, you know, reader, you can see them over
Dubuque.
    All those families in American fiction
who have had money & lost it, cash accounts rolling away
like cartwheels,
are beautiful in a lush & melodramatic way.
        I'm not
thinking of Hatty Greene, the plum tree girl, who went crazy,
so much as the various family novels.
        Midwestern or
otherwise. They get to me.
The mothers & fathers & the family pictures.
Even horses are touched & amazed by visions of lost
newspapers, women who take their children to the grandmother's
church,
    headwaiters who knew *my* grandfather by his last name
& called him Mr. Cant & shook hands
as he left the club.
        To do what? To go home & sit alone
in the living room of his large-frame house, drink a double scotch
or bourbon, & think of his beautiful wife who had died 2 weeks
after jubilant childbirth.

2.

And there was my mother a few weeks old upstairs in a
wicker bassinet with a housekeeper who complained
about her feet.

3.

But now reality has finally bled its sweet light
into my dark head, & it is obvious that those blue moons
over Dubuque are illusory.

4.

Making money back is more difficult
than getting it in the first place.
(Fame & success are
attractive
but a lush magazine office seems less likely today than a 20-acre
farm with fresh hay.)

Nobody in my immediate family was ever sumptuously well paid except for Duncan.
My exacting father taught Greek Literature in his grey tweed suit
for $2800 a year during the Depression.

5.

My
mother missed her inheritance by one elegant black pump.

6.

Money is everywhere & always in different hands. The un-
employed, for example,
used to come to our back door in St.
Mary's before I was born, & my mother would give them soup
from as far away as Halifax
or Prince Rupert.
I can never remember the faces of these men

when I try to think of them because they stopped passing through

the year I was born. That was the end of the Depression. The long
slow looping
migrations of shirt-sleeved men & freight cars & hobo camps.
                                                    And then
a few months later, I was sitting in the middle of my parents'
living room at 92 Wellington & crowing like a rooster.
                                                    I ate
the same bread & soup they did. But I could never
remember the faces of those men,
                              who perhaps slept under a moon
until the factories, Massey-Harris,
                              Swift's, Canada Packers,
Imperial Carpet, General Motors,
                              opened up
& they found jobs. Perhaps my mother missed them sometimes
when she went to the back door to let the dog out
or throw breadcrumbs to the robins. They stopped coming

at the end of the Depression.

                              7.

              I love Canada Malting Ltd. for the bold way
it juts out into the Lake at the foot of Bathurst, but
blue moons or otherwise, my mother & Hatty Greene
were totally different.
                    Hatty Greene had buckets of coppers
& quarters under her sink. Wads of Jeffersons under the
mattress.

8.

My mother thought
money grew on trees. She was very good on the names of flowers
& shrubs, & perfect in almost every way.
But she never photographed anything herself, or studied
the photographs she'd kept of White Plains or Dubuque
since childhood.

9.

She didn't give a flying flounce
for bank notes or property deeds. A broken Scottish grandfather's
clock she kept. Sure. It was
lovely.

10.

But she gave away our house,
9 big rooms, plus a
garage you could have put a 5-piece band in it with Lena Horne
singing "Don't You Magnolia Me,"
                              to the first stranger
who offered to help her hoe the garden, or take the ½-ton blue
pickup out for a drive in the country.

Blue Skies & Opera

I think it's almost a purer shade of blue than my memory,
extraordinarily even & consistent,
pellucid means something else,
maybe lucid,
      is "lucent" a real *OED* word,
not warm,
      not cold,
well,
      you know, it all depends on the sun,

a solar angle gone askew can change anything in a love affair,
last night's moon
was an extraordinary sickle dazzling its way over far western traffic,
all those millions of seal beams buzzing along the darkness of Bloor St. at night,

a good solar angle, excellent, so nothing is going off-centre, yet, Rodolfo,

I'm listening to Puccini's *La Bohème* with Susanna Philips as Musetta,
I'm on iPod, I'm outside in the January sun,
I'm on Cappuccino from Mercurio down the street,
you know,
Musetta, still attractive, fleshly, a tad whorish, loudly dressed,
going after other men, throwing chamber pots at the head of Marcello,

they're bringing the principals out onstage now,
after all, this is a famous opera that has lasted well over a hundred years,
eat your heart out, Gore Vidal
      I shouldn't be so literal in these poems, 2009.
Why not?
      As if the whole world is at this moment illuminated by a gentle sun,

making the Felliniesque tall white condo building across the street
seem like the height of glamour, well, some interesting marketing people,
I think how wonderful it would be to sail across the sky in a twin-engine Otter,
probably very St. Exupéry & sexual & dangerous at the same time,
here on the ground, fresh from the chiropractor, looking at this sky, 1:55 pm,
I feel that I could & can aha aha . . . live forever on pure oxygen.

Jaffa Oranges Are Sweet

Daily life, oranges, the significance of red lentil soup.
Pizza with ice cream late at night with friends.

I'm interested in too wide a variety of subjects,
Absalom, Absalom!;
Go Down, Moses,
the collected stories of Truman Capote,
I want to see Bertolucci's *The Last Emperor* again,
CDs to buy, okay,
first of all I have to look at my budget,
Lilo Biali is on the top list,
here's a little night music contrast, Renée
Fleming's fabulous disc called *Divas,*

I'm walking on the golden splinters of heaven's floor.
Open the windows, shut the door.
Of course I'm interested in folklore but not very much.
Remarkable women of the '60s.
There were a lot of them & they're all on film.
Diane Keaton, Katharine Ross & Grace Slick from Jefferson Airplane.
What a man needs is an understanding of *Here* & *Now,*
A man needs loving arms. O Crazy Arms,
not to be confused with Neil Young's *Crazy Horse.*
In the spirit of Diane Keaton.
I have seen the best minds of my generation come out of the closet
& link up with a male partner & move to San Francisco.
Not me, sorry, Pauley, I'm wired for women;
Women & contemporary myths & where to shop.
The cranes are flying & I'm eating strawberry cheesecake

at a little diner called *Billy's* & I think confidence is just
a question of what you've had for breakfast.

Amazing & Innocent

How much I love the tall Heinz ketchup bottle
sitting
       absolutely innocent   on my kitchen table

with its white cap, opaque, the neat red 10 pt red letters Heinz
& the small red arrow
           showing us   in the great darkness
of our unbelievable innocence
where & how to turn the cap   Just one turn does it, Mr. Heinz

It's amazing & it's innocent & it's ⅘ full & what's more
I just had some
with my quiet Wednesday evening supper of lean ground beef
radicchio
      & small white potatoes

Caricature

Everybody knows that famous cartoon
or caricature
or maybe it's an india ink & pencil drawing by some fashion
artist on exhibit somewhere that I'm thinking
of —
        a beautiful young woman with blonde hair cut in a
flip
& a black nothing dress
bare-shouldered
beautiful graceful shoulders

& she has a large block of ice sitting on her left shoulder
& a casual smile

she's wearing nothing except for a smile & a block of ice

& of course, the black nothing dress

& pumps — or running shoes.   And there I am in this cartoon
or caricature
standing off to one side with a big sheepish look on my
otherwise more or less handsome face
& a rumpled chocolate brown gabardine suit. That's exactly
how you made me feel for a long time — O, I don't know,

4 or 5 years — whenever we bumped into each other
at a party at some friend's or
occasionally in a restaurant like Fenton's
La Folie where I had lunch with my mother once
as late as 1976, but which I generally wouldn't go to

with friends even though I had a little money
or *Noodles* — Stephen & Barry & I liked *Noodles* a lot.
& you would stare at me casually
insolently over the block of ice & say, How are you, David,
and then nothing but frozen air. Now the block of ice is gone.
You're friendly, some people might say cool.
But you're interested, you read my books.
I have that lovely feeling of having just thrown a no-hitter against New York.

Driving All the Way to Tibet

Truth. I'm not a very good driver. I should at least fly
Toronto –
      Paris
do the Luxembourg Gardens where Rilke wrote
his wonderful poem about the panther
restlessness
& the mictating membrane, I should fly — with that poem
in my flight luggage — to Llasa in central Tibet. The central
plains area. That's where the Great Monastery is and various
Dalai Lamas have come & gone some of them very young & more
resplendently dressed than others.

      But I don't.

They have red roofs in Tibet.
They have slate roofs in Tibet — some houses have tiles
at the front & some houses don't. They think yak meat is more
tasty than chicken or rare western steak in Tibet. They don't
really want your Pizza Pizza in Tibet. Or your dill & sour cream
potato chips. The girls in Tibet have unbelievably sweet breath.
I think most of the boys are probably polite
unlike the street toughs that turn up on the arts committee
at the Library readings program in Toronto. They have a work ethic
in Tibet, O I'm sure they do. I'm sure they would find me undisciplined.
The monks do extraordinary things in the great temple.
O I'm sure they do.

      But I don't go. I stay here & wrestle
with western culture. My friend Frank thinks I'm crazy, if Ira
Gershwin were alive he would say you're a beautiful guy, I think

I understand you, you're a schlemiel, but what a high I.Q.

It's my anima. I love everything.

You

Kissing you is like walking naked through a field
of soft corn as tall as my eye.

                              Your eyes
are blue.

Trends That Didn't Start in America

Cubism, for example, those deconstructed blue
violins
& brown table menus didn't come into the world
in South Dakota. They began in Paris, & the French cities
in Provence didn't know anything about it for years. Poker

began in England, maybe in France, maybe in Italy. The Hula-
hoop
was first introduced as a gymnastic training aid in German
high schools sometime before World War 1. Alexander Graham
Bell
        invented the telephone (although Francis Ford Coppola
has a character in a street demonstration
claim that it was invented by somebody called Mucci) but Xerox
& schmaltz herring were both invented
in Sweden. Da Vinci,
                        with his camera obscura, obviously invented
the basic principles of the modern camera. For some reason

it all makes me think of Stevie Wonder, age 14, prox.
taking on & reinventing a classic blues, "Put on your red dress, baby,"
I'm going to take you out tonight
                        now that is American
& Georgia O'Keeffe's paintings are American
& Stieglitz's photographs are American
& I want that same authenticity in all of my work —
American at this epicentre of Toronto
as opposed to somewhere in L.A. or Mississippi. And Stevie Wonder,

at the age of 14 or so, the whole personal (not national) factor,

that is just so astounding.
                    I'm not so crazy about recent Wonder,

but that early work blows me away & gathers me up.
That's the kind of music we make when we kiss,
use it all & use it well with your eyes wide open.

Painters Who Were Not Exactly Put Out of Business
by Jackson Pollock's Relative Success in 1942

Vermeer et al., various Dutch interiorists, the Van Gogh
of the olive trees at Arles, Thos. Eakins. Especially that great
painting of the Operating Theatre. Velasquez and all those wonderful
muddy browns. Even the ability to render Aesop's face so perfectly. Think
for a moment of those women in the *Turkish Bath* by Ingres they are a cross-
section of the most intelligent women in Paris. Persian miniatures of which
there are many actually there are probably millions. Picasso's Blue Period
the young jugglers, various pink acrobats, & the boy leading the horse
without a bridle into a blue space that appears before us the fortunate
viewer, Cézanne and the barns. I have recanted a bit in my views on Cézanne,
Giotto, Fantin-Latour, Hals, Matthew Brady, Alfred Stieglitz, Edward
Steichen. Edward Hopper although I keep associating him with Dennis
Hopper who I have to admit I also like, even if he does look excessively
handsome with that beautiful blond baby son in the Herb Ritts GAP ad
featured for my pleasure the other day at one of my favourite subway stops Miro.
Which reminds me of the story in which Robert McAlmon mistook Miro (McAlmon
was glib not stupid & wrote *Being Geniuses Together*) for Hemingway's valet, because
Miro c/w dark bowler & dark suit, was walking with H outside of Closerie
des Lilas carrying H's gym bag as a favour. Almost all the paintings
of Francis Bacon, although I don't really believe Bacon is a great painter,
Sigmar Polke the German post-abstractionist painter who likes going to
receptions wearing a towel, he's a very fine, perhaps really brilliant
painter. Jim Dine's sinks because they are such beautiful sinks.

The Great Philosphers Don't Listen to Enough Coltrane

The great philosophers are all wrong.
Tu Fu,
    a wonderful Chinese poet
from long before Schopenhauer or Ludwig Wittgenstein —
said everything
when he simply said,
              Look at the moon.

O the moon. I am like a young bull calf out in the fields
of the moon. Or
              a bottle of wine
& the moon.
That sounds good. Eggplant is a wonderful vegetable.
The Greeks
call it "the testicles of Christ." That's a good phrase,

the New Testament
is certainly a ballsy book. I would like to consider
some of these abstract questions
in greater detail
but what I want most is eggplant with parmesan
& tomato sauce. Or
              marinate some bite-sized chunks
perhaps,
       & have them with chicken & fettuccine.

Computer Files

Tod is 15 years old,
             tall for his age & slim,
sandy brown hair, diffident, high IQ. Tod handles school work
easily,
        his approach to taking notes & participating in class
is casual & easy to get along with.
                          Geography
doesn't inspire him, he's fun, good personality

likes physics, math & Iggy Pop singing "Louie, Louie."

Diffident, unusually high IQ, he almost failed English
but that's because the teacher didn't like his story
about the Metro Zoo. The hippo was totally bizarre.
                 The hippo was totally bizarre,
the birds were amazing,
he & his girlfriend Kris hadn't expected so many birds.

Tod is tall for his age & slim,
sandy brown hair, diffident, high IQ, easy to get along with,

likes Iggy Pop singing "Louie, Louie"
& isn't sure if he should pre-register for a physics major
or if he might like to spend several years studying
biology or animal behaviouralism.

Rust Never Sleeps

Am I in a rut these days or in a groove? Dunno.
Get in the groove
                & let the good times roll.

I was on my way down to the Robarts Library
& this extraordinary girl came walking past my camera.
O stop, I said, stop in the name of love.
And when I got to the Library they didn't have the book
anyway. So diddle,
              fiddle, that's what Pinkus Zuckerman
who is in lots of hot water at the NAC these days
calls his violin. Good name. Anyway, which is what
I began to say. The word rut makes me think of rust.
Rust never sleeps. Good title, Neil, I also am searching
O searching
        O searching
               for a heart of gold
but you will only find that heart of gold if you look
into yourself deeply & find the secret of the golden flower.
Rut? O yes, rut. Dogs rut. Well, no, I am not a dog or a hog.
Groove turns up again & again in FM discussions
of new recent African world/beat. Hosts talk a lot
about Cuban/Afro fusing with Brazilian & picking up
some reggae en route to the market. What I find —
& look OK I don't have a Ph.D. in music
                     but —
is a very essentialized & danceable as hell version
of what some of the baroque cats were doing in the 1690s.

Afrika/Afrique

A chocolate company in West Germany produced a new
product,
        a chocolate wafer biscuit, small squares,

coated with a good dark chocolate

saleable for a reasonable price, in marks or francs or dollars,

they had a perfect good simple idea for the package design
but they needed
a name for this new biscuit. Just as they were sitting

around across the street from company HQ, in a small café,
having some kaffe & a small strudel,

a beautiful young African girl came walking past,
about 20, maybe, 5'6", slim, a bit like Makeba at 20

or a bit like the girl from Ipanema. "Good," says the VP
of advertising,
        "that's our inspiration for today. Let's call
this product Afrika." It was done — a *fait accompli*,

for sure. I bought a package, thousands of miles away,
& tested, well, let's say, I ate 3 or 4. A bit small,
I thought, good marks for the wafer construction

not huge marks for the chocolate which actually I thought
seemed a bit like belgische but not expensive belgische.

As for the girl, O she was stunning, amazing, fantabulous,

I would prefer the girl, & some coffee & a brioche.

A Couple of Interesting Brothers

      Paul & Joseph Montgolfier were always trying to get high,
not amyl nitrate,
              the whole giant steps routine,
no,
      Paul & Joseph wanted to get high up in the air
& get a good look at what was going on over "there" in the New World,
or for that matter, across the channel. Was George III really mad,

or was he just playing around with medications
for his so-called variegate porphyria?
So they built an aerial balloon, large & original.

      They used taffeta & 1800 buttons,
obviously the air is going to escape at a certain point
but not before altitude.

      On July 16, 1783
they took to the air with a sheep, a duck & a rooster
& achieved 324 feet in 15 seconds. It was a record.

      People searching for profound starting points take note.
Their original idea was laundry
drying over a fire.

Geraldine

                                    The critics didn't
think she was very good in Alan Rudolf's *Welcome to L.A.*
but I thought she
                    was fabulous, she was moody & beautiful
& angsty & I thought the single nude scene was stark &
isolated & in good taste. Taste is everything,
they say, taste is important. Somebody in London
said that a long time ago; and somebody in New York said,
Well, yes, but taste is a matter of taste. I'm glad
That George Santayana didn't become a language philosopher.
He was too intelligent, too interested in the world too full of
exuberant spirits. Salubrious. Celerity. The wages for bad
writing like some recent Updike — well up you too & up U2 — are
obscurity. He's definitely obscure in my living room. And the
salary for intelligence is love. OK. We're agreed on this.
The salary for intelligence is love. My mother used to love
long graceful stalks of celery fresh from the cold water tap
with just a touch of salt & stuffed with pimento cream cheese.
Sounds cheesy to you? Well, that's you, she was divine,
she was just simply a gorgeous woman,
and she loved it. Also sandwiches made with fresh whole wheat
bread lightly buttered & gently packed with sliced green olives.
She was interesting, more beautiful perhaps than that girl
in *Welcome to L.A.* but not angsty. And generally speaking, she
didn't do nude scenes.

Gerald Murphy

I like the way that Gerald Murphy describes
his life
    in *Living Well Is the Best Revenge*.
How he came to a certain point   before he was 35
where he decided that he couldn't see any point
to doing anything except
simply appreciating the very best. But sure, it becomes
semantics if you stop and think about it.
                            What difference
would there be for us
if he were to say Things of great beauty; as opposed
to
Fine Living?   I mean, look, Fine Living sounds to me
like a guy sitting in a large empty living room
holding the same large glass of 1924 Pinot Noir
up to his nose again & again.   So, your net result
would probably be — decadent & haughty. Something
like that. But
             Things of great beauty. Ah, that's good.
They entertained a lot. His wife was beautiful. Their
children were fucking
bright & heartbreakingly adorable. They entertained Scott
& Zelda & Jean Cocteau & Picasso. Even then,
Picasso only had one name. He was that famous. To
die for. A variety of beautiful young men had
just done that in the first world war. They
never entertained Virginia Woolf.
                      Americans went to France.
Virginia stayed in London. Hoover ushered in the Depression.
Hemingway went to the Louvre early in the morning after it

opened with its morning hours & looked at the Cézannes
on an empty stomach with 2 café au laits, "tangible paint,"
a man wrestling with perspectives & proportions,
& it impressed him. Gerald Murphy rarely came to Paris. He
loved the beach at Nice. He loved the water.

North of 60

Last week, on a calm October day,
Mervin Good Eagle hanged himself from a tree in Sandy Bay,
Sask. He
was 19, medium height, fairly good looking, no apparent problems.
He
was one of the stars of a very successful show, *North of 60*.
Maybe he was tired of doing other people's scripts.
Maybe he was a gay guy in a straight male's body.
We don't know how he looked out and saw us,
so obviously we don't really know Mervin as he saw himself.
We saw him on the show as boyish,
boyish, good-natured, and somewhat reflective.
Not a bad part to play, and well-paid. He was a role model
for others, that's for sure.
It was foolish, but probably didn't take very long.
His girlfriend Mildred Bear came down from her house
and found him hanging from the tree.
What can anybody say that makes very much sense?
Listen Mildred, there is only one thing I can say,
maybe eagles don't speak, they spread their wings and soar.
I don't know much about eagles. I've seen some
but they didn't speak. When they tilt — they can see the whole world
out of the corner of one eye. It says in the Bible that eagles soar
and angels descend. When the bear clutched Marian Engel's thigh
she dropped her duffel bag
and the bear kissed the subtle white inside of her neck.
Angels are aliens in spaceships. Angels descend
and eagles soar. I am not an eagle. If I were an angel I would descend
and give you all the bread of happiness
the salt of anger

& the message you already know better than I know
The moon & the lakes & the hills
are forever.

Einstein & Daily Life

         Einstein was a sort of idiot savant. Didn't know Jack
Daniel's
       about philosophy, or anthropology, or sociology or psych.
He was a lovely old man with milk-white hair
& striking blue eyes.
         He published *A Special Theory*
of Relativity in 1905,
           $E = mc^2$, in the lang. of physics,
Didn't know zilch about *Tom Sawyer* or *Crime and Punishment* by Dostoyevsky.
Don't get me wrong.
I think he was good at what he did.
                Einstein never went
to an Alfred Jarry play in his life
& as far as I know had never heard of Alban Berg

who wrote that wonderful opera *Lulu* & then committed suicide some time after
the Nazis came
to power in 1933.

Physics talks a lot about photons & the speed of light, true,
but it doesn't tell us anything about relativity in our
daily life.

Or *Jude the Obscure* or Proust or Erik Satie.